Bats

Elizabeth Carney

NATIONAL GEOGRAPHIC
Washington, D.C.

For Cheri and Raquel, and the
fond memories of our
nighttime mischief.
- E.C.

Library of Congress Cataloging-in-Publication Data

Carney, Elizabeth, 1981-
Bats / by Elizabeth Carney.
p. cm.
ISBN 978-1-4263-0710-2 (pbk. : alk. paper) -- ISBN 978-1-4263-0711-9 (library binding : alk. paper)
1. Bats--Juvenile literature. I. Title.
QL737.C5C348 2010
599.4--dc22
2010011636

Cover, Theo Allofs; 1, Martin Withers/ FLPA/ Minden Pictures/ NationalGeographicStock.com; 2, Merlin D. Tuttle, Bat Conservation International; 5, cbimages/ Alamy; 6, Norbert Wu/ Minden Pictures/ NationalGeographicStock.com; 8, Michael Lynch/ Alamy; 9, Carol Farneti Foster/ Getty Images; 10, Tim Laman/ NationalGeographicStock.com; 12, Mark Carwardine/ naturepl.com; 13, Eric Baccega/ naturepl.com; 14, Victor Habbick Visions/ Photo Researchers, Inc.; 16 (top), ImageState/ Alamy; 16 (bottom), Dr. Morley Read/ Shutterstock; 17 (top), Barry Mansell/ naturepl.com; 17 (bottom), Nina Leen/ Time & Life Pictures Creative/ Getty Images; 19, Theo Allofs/ The Image Bank/ Getty Images; 21, Tristan Savatier/ Flickr/ Getty Images; 22, WIN-Initiative/ Getty Images; 23, Dr. Merlin D. Tuttle/ Bat Conservation International/ Photo Researchers, Inc.; 24, Newspix/ Rex USA; 26, Michael & Patricia Fogden/ Minden Pictures/ NationalGeographicStock.com; 28, Ingo Arndt/ Foto Natura/ Minden Pictures/ /NationalGeographicStock.com; 29 (top), Tom Uhlman/ Alamy; 29 (middle), Oxford Scientific/ Photolibrary/ Getty Images; 29 (bottom), Nick Gordon/ ardea.com; 30, Tim Laman/ NationalGeographicStock.com; 30 (inset), Steve Downer/ ardea.com; 31 (top), Konrad Wothe/ Minden Pictures/ National-GeographicStock.com; 31 (middle), Chris Howes/ Wild Places Photography/ Alamy; 31 (bottom), Hugo Willcox/ Foto Natura Minden Pictures/ NationalGeographicStock.com; 2, (top, left) ; 32 (middle, left), Bob Stefko/ The Image Bank/ Getty Images; 32 (bottom, left), Tim Laman/ NationalGeographicStock.com; 32 (top, right), Victor Habbick Visions/ Photo Researchers, Inc.; 32 (middle, right), Michael & Patricia Fogden/ NationalGeographicStock.com; 32 (bottom, right), Steffen & Alexandra Sailer/ ardea.com.

Printed in the United States of America
(RLB) 12/WOR/2

Table of Contents

2330

What's a Bat?

I sleep by day. I fly by night. I have no feathers to aid my flight. What am I?

The answer is a bat! A bat is a mammal. Mammals are animals that nurse their young, have hair, and are warm-blooded. Humans, dogs, and whales are all mammals. But bats have a special ability. They can fly!

Bat Words

MAMMAL: A warm-blooded animal that drinks its mother's milk, has a backbone, and has hair

Flying fox bats

Bat Food

There are about 1,200 types of bats in the world. Most of them eat insects. Insect–eating bats are usually small in size.

There are more than 150 types of fruit bats. These bats are usually larger and search for sweet fruits and other plants.

Q Why don't bats live alone?

A They prefer to hang out with their friends.

Silky short-tailed bat feeding

A few bats hunt for larger prey, such as frogs, birds, or mice.

Some people think all bats suck your blood. This is not true. Only three kinds of bats drink blood. This group is known as vampire bats. They mostly feed on the blood of animals like cows and deer—not humans.

Vampire bat

Fringed lip bat
eating a frog

Night Flight

Did you know that while you're
fast asleep, bats are busy filling their
bellies? Bats are nocturnal, meaning
they're active at night. This way
of life has many advantages for a
bat. Insect-eating bats often feast

Thousands of wrinkled-lipped bats leaving a cave at dusk

on bugs that come out after dark. Pollen- and nectar-eating bats might feed on plants that only open at night. Nectar is a sweet liquid made by flowers.

Bat Words

NOCTURNAL: The state of being active at night

NECTAR: A sweet liquid made by flowers

Bat Bodies

Scientists call bats Chiroptera (kir–OP–ter–a), a Greek name that means "hand wing." That's because bats have four fingers and a thumb just like us. A thin layer of skin connects the fingers. This forms a wing. Bats also have a sensitive nose and big ears. Their big ears help some bats see with sound!

Q What did the bat say when its buddy asked, "What's up?"

A "The ground."

Coat of fur

Four fingers

Thumb

Sensitive nose

Big ears

Sharp eyesight

Wing

13

Bat Words

ECHOLOCATION: A system in some animals for locating objects using sound waves

In the pitch-black night, bats can scoop up a tiny insect with ease. No flashlight required! How do they do it? They make a sound that travels until it hits an object. Then, it bounces off the object and travels back to the bat. From this echo the bat can tell an object's size and how far away it is. This is called echolocation.

Funny Face

Amazonian bat

False vampire bat

Some bats have strange-looking faces. Special ears, noses, and mouths help bats tune into and make sounds while they use echolocation.

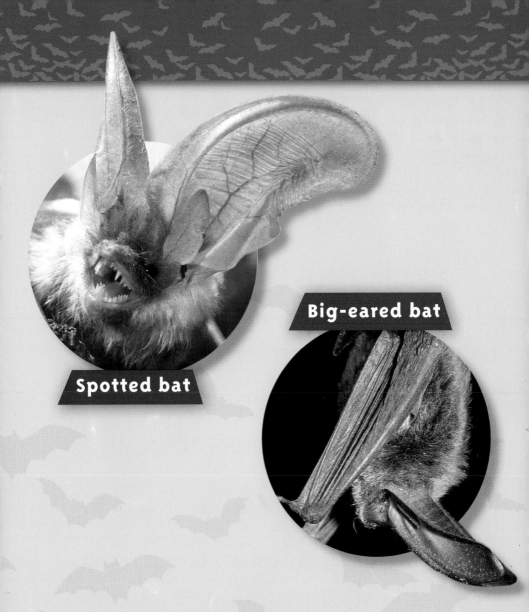

Spotted bat

Big-eared bat

Their faces may look
odd to us, but for bats, their
features work perfectly!

Hanging Out

When bats are not hunting for food, they're usually hiding in a roost. Roosts can be caves, treetops, or attics. Bats pick places that are well hidden and protect them from bad weather.

When most bats rest in their roost, they hang upside down!

Bat Words

ROOST: The place where animals such as bats and certain types of birds rest

Little redheaded flying foxes roosting in a tree

Have you ever hung upside down in a jungle gym? You might start to feel dizzy. Bats have special veins to keep their blood flowing properly so they never feel dizzy.

Bats can't take off from the ground like birds do. They have to fall into flight. Hanging upside down is the best way to make a quick getaway.

Bats hanging and flying in cave

21

Baby Bats

Mother and
baby bat

Gambian epauletted bat mother and baby flying

Baby bats, called pups, completely depend on their mothers after they're born. They're blind, hairless, and can't fly. They cling to their mother's fur. The pups nurse their mother's milk until their wings are strong enough to fly.

Bat Rescue

During storms in an Australian rain forest, wind can knock baby bats to the forest floor. The babies usually don't survive unless wildlife workers come to the rescue. The lucky bats

are taken to a bat hospital. The babies
are bundled in blankets and fed milk
from a bottle. After a few months,
they are strong enough to return to
the wild.

Nature's Helpers

Hairy-legged nectar bat with pollen on head and shoulders

A world without bats wouldn't be very nice. Bats are an important part of the ecosystem. Insect-eating bats gobble up millions of bugs. Many of these insects are pests that could harm humans or destroy crops. Bats keep their numbers under control.

Other bats keep forests healthy by spreading seeds and pollen. This allows trees and flowers to multiply.

Bat Words

ECOSYSTEM: The environment in which living things live

Bat Myths Busted!

MYTH: Bats are blind.
TRUTH: Bats have excellent eyesight. Some bats hunt using sight alone.

Some people have misunderstandings about bats. Here are a few common myths that drive experts batty.

MYTH: Bats are dirty.
TRUTH: Bats are actually neat freaks. They groom themselves frequently. Mothers lick their babies to keep them clean.

MYTH: Bats get stuck in hair.
TRUTH: With sharp senses and echolocation, bats are very good fliers. They can avoid obstacles the width of a thread.

MYTH: Vampire bats turn into human vampires.
TRUTH: There is no such thing as a human vampire, and bats certainly don't turn into them.

Bat Hall of Fame

TEENIE TINY

The smallest bat in the world is the bumblebee bat. Its wingspan is five inches across. Its body is the size of a jelly bean.

MEGA WINGS

The largest bat is the three-pound flying fox. Its wingspan can be 6 feet long. That's longer than you are tall!

HAPPY CAMPER

The Hondurian white bat makes tents out of leaves to protect itself from constant rain showers.

MOST CROWDED HOME

20 million Mexican free-tailed bats live in one Texas cave. These bats are also the fanciest fliers. They can soar as high as 10,000 feet and zoom through the air at speeds over 40 miles an hour!

BIGGEST APPETITE

Little brown bats can eat up to 1,200 mosquitoes in one night! Yum!

MAMMAL: A warm-blooded animal that nurses its young, has a backbone and hair

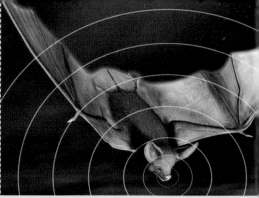

ECHOLOCATION: A system in some animals for locating objects using sound waves

ROOST: The place where animals such as bats and certain types of birds rest

NECTAR: A sweet liquid made by flowers

NOCTURNAL: The state of being active at night

ECOSYSTEM: The environment in which living things live